All inquiries should be addressed to:
Barron's Educational Series, Inc.
250 Wireless Boulevard, Hauppauge, NY 11788
http://www.barronseduc.com

Library of Congress Catalog Card No. **99 - 66378**

International Standard Book No. 0-7641-1461-1

Printed in China

Stop Picking on Me

A FIRST LOOK AT BULLYING

PAT THOMAS
ILLUSTRATED BY LESLEY HARKER

BARRON'S

Some of these children are bullies.
Can you tell which ones?

Bullies look just like everyone else but they don't act like everyone else.

Bullies enjoy hurting other people and
making them do what they say.

The only way they know how to get
what they want is by being cruel.

Bullies don't always hurt your body—they can hurt your feelings as well. A bully can make you feel like it's your fault that they are picking on you, even though this isn't true.

What about you?

Do you know anyone who is a bully?
What sort of things do they do?

Anyone can be a bully.
It could be a boy or a girl,
a person on their own or
in a gang.

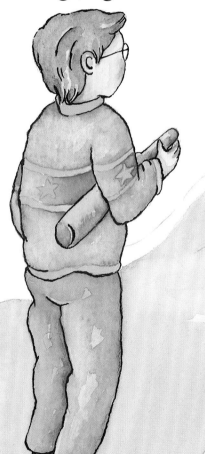

It can even be an adult. A bully
can pick on you or leave you out
of games and groups.

At some time in their lives, most people have hurt someone else, without meaning to, by acting like a bully. But some people act this way all the time.

Bullies never have a good reason for hurting other people. Often they pick on anyone they think is different from them.

Some bullies pick on people who
are a different size from them or whose skin is
a different color. Some bullies will even pick on you
because of the clothes you are wearing.

Kids who act like bullies have probably
been bullied themselves, sometimes by
other children.

Sometimes their parents or other adults may have been cruel to them. This is very sad, but it is never a good reason for being unkind to others.

Bullies don't like themselves very much. This makes it hard for them to like other people and treat them well.

The only way bullies can like themselves is to pick on others. Doing this makes them feel more powerful.

We all need to feel loved. That is why being bullied hurts so much. When someone is bullying you, it can make you feel scared or angry, miserable or hurt.

You may not want to sleep, or when you do sleep you may have nightmares. You may not feel like eating or going to school anymore.

What about you?

Everyone feels differently about being bullied.
Have you ever been bullied?
How did it make you feel?

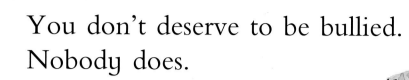

You don't deserve to be bullied.
Nobody does.

One of the hardest
things to learn is how to
deal with a bully without becoming
a bully yourself. Hitting back or being
cruel usually only makes the problem worse.

What about you?

What sort of things do you do when someone bullies you? Can you think of any different ways to deal with a bully?

A good way to stop bullying is to talk to someone about it. This can be a parent or a teacher or any grown-up you feel comfortable with.

You may not want
to talk to anyone
about it, but
you should.

All bullies hope that their victims won't tell
on them. Keeping it to yourself lets a bully
know that it's all right to go on hurting you.

Another way to stop bullies is to let the people who love you help. Other people's love can help you feel good about yourself and reassure you that it's not your fault if you are bullied.

Bullies only pick on people they know they can hurt. Feeling good about yourself and liking yourself is probably the best way to stop them.

Also, when you feel good about yourself
you do not need to bully others
to get what you want.

That's important to remember because
the fewer bullies there are in our world, the
better place it will be for all of us to live in.

HOW TO USE THIS BOOK

A bullied child will have many powerful feelings – don't let these panic or overwhelm you. A bullied child needs unconditional love first and foremost. If you try to make it better – for instance, make your child less unhappy, less angry, or less scared – you are not accepting your child's feelings. You can make your children more confident by giving them the freedom to express their feelings.

When your child is being bullied it can sometimes bring up powerful memories of being bullied yourself. When your child is a victim, it makes you a victim too, and this is very frightening for many adults. Try not to work unresolved feelings out through your child. Don't make your child fight the bully you wish you had fought, or say what you wish you had said.

Children learn how to behave at home. If your child is involved in bullying others it is a good time to look objectively at the way they are being treated at home and the way various family members interact with each other.

Schools are in a powerful position to stamp out bullying. Those schools with a zero tolerance for bullying generally have the lowest rates of bullying behavior among students. The "bully box," where children can report bullying anonymously, should be a part of every school.

Individual classes can also help to promote discussion about bullying. A useful way to do this is through role playing. Children in the class should be given the opportunity through short improvisations to act out both the role of the bully and the bullied in front of the class. Group discussion can then take place about how it feels to be bullied, how best to cope with bullying, and what to do if you are being bullied.

BOOKS TO READ

For Children

We Can Get Along
Lauren Murphy Payne (Free Spirit Publishing, 1997)

The Berenstain Bears and Too Much Teasing
Stan and Jan Berenstain (Random House, 1995)

The Berenstain Bears and the Bully
Stan and Jan Berenstain (Random House, 1993)

Bullies Are a Pain in the Brain
Trevor Romain (Free Spirit Publishing, 1997)

For Adults

Caring for Your School-Age Child, Ages 5 to 12
Edward L. Schor, M.D. (Bantam, 1997)

USEFUL CONTACT

Parents Anonymous
675 West Foothill Blvd.
Suite 220
Claremont, CA 91711-3416
(909) 621-6184
*Works for the prevention and treatment of child abuse. Publishes two free
newsletters. With 31 state and 1200 local groups, the organization may
be listed in your local phone directory.*